P9-CDV-047

Garden Fresh Recipes

Homemade Recipes for Homegrown Foods

Cookbook Resources, LLC
Highland Village, Texas

Garden Fresh Recipes
Homemade Recipes for Homegrown Foods

Printed September 2012

© Copyright 2011 by Cookbook Resources, LLC

All Rights Reserved.

No part of this book may be reproduced in any form without
written permission from the publisher, except for brief passages
included in a review appearing in a newspaper or magazine with
permission from the publisher.

International Standard Book Number: 978-1-59769-105-5

Library of Congress Control Number: 2011043266

Library of Congress Cataloging-in-Publication Data:

    Garden fresh recipes : homemade recipes for homegrown
    foods. -- 1st ed.
      p. cm.
   Includes bibliographical references and index.
   ISBN 978-1-59769-105-5
  1. Cooking (Vegetables) 2. Vegetable gardening.
  3. Kitchen gardens.
  TX801.G38 2012
  641.6'5--dc23

                       2011043266

Cover and design by Rasor Design

Edited, Designed and Published in the United States of America
and Manufactured in China by
Cookbook Resources, LLC
541 Doubletree Drive
Highland Village, Texas 75077

Toll free 866-229-2665

www.cookbookresources.com

Bringing Family and Friends to the Table

Garden Fresh Recipes

Easy, delicious, family-favorite recipes for foods straight from the garden can make family meals special occasions. Know where your food comes from… grow it yourself or buy it from local farmers for the best flavors and quality.

We hope you enjoy…

★ the best recipes for fresh fruits and vegetables.

★ specially selected recipes for quick-and-easy preparation with everyday ingredients.

★ inexpensive ways to serve high-quality fresh foods.

★ knowing where your food comes from.

Bringing Family and Friends to the Table

We recognize the importance of shared meals as a means of building family bonds with memories and traditions that will last a lifetime. At mealtimes we share more than food. We share ourselves.

This cookbook is dedicated with gratitude and respect to all those who show their love by making home-cooked meals and bringing family and friends to the table.

The Editor

More statistical studies are finding that family meals play a significant role in childhood development. Children who eat with their families four or more nights per week are healthier, make better grades in school, score higher on aptitude tests and are less likely to have problems with drugs.

Contents

Recipes

Contents
Recipes — continued

Fresh Tomato Salsa

4 medium tomatoes, diced
2 - 4 green onions with tops, diced
1 - 2 jalapeno peppers
½ cup snipped cilantro leaves
Juice of 1 small lime
1 teaspoon sugar

- Dice tomatoes and onions in large bowl to save juices. Wear gloves to remove stems and seeds from jalapenos and dry with paper towels. Dice jalapenos and add to tomatoes.

- Combine with all other ingredients and 1 teaspoon salt and refrigerate for about 15 to 20 minutes.

- Remove from refrigerator and taste. If tomatoes are too tart, add a little sugar to sweeten. Refrigerate for about 30 minutes more to blend flavors before serving. Makes 1½ cups.

We're always the same age on the inside.
–Gertrude Stein

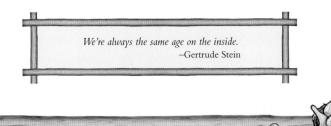

Tropical Mango Salsa

Serve with grilled pork or swordfish or tuna steaks or even with bruschetta for a tasty appetizer.

2 large very ripe mangoes, peeled, cubed
½ cup diced purple onion
¼ cup chopped fresh cilantro
2 - 3 tablespoons freshly squeezed lime juice

- Stir together all ingredients. Cover salsa with plastic wrap.

- Refrigerate for 30 minutes to blend flavors. Makes about 1 cup.

TIP: Bell peppers, green onions or pineapple are good mixed with mango, too.

> The most interesting information comes from children, for they tell all they know and then stop.
> –Mark Twain

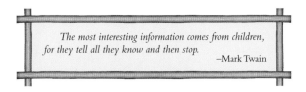

Cilantro Pico de Gallo

1 whole jalapeno, seeded, diced*
½ cup minced fresh cilantro
1 bunch green onions with tops, chopped
2 large tomatoes, chopped
Juice of 2 limes
½ teaspoon garlic salt
½ teaspoon seasoned salt

Stir together all ingredients and ¼ teaspoon pepper or to taste. Cover and refrigerate to blend flavors.

Serve with tortilla chips, over guacamole salad or over grilled fish or pork. Makes about 1 cup.

*TIP: Wear rubber gloves when removing seeds from jalapenos.

> Children who eat at home almost every night during the week are more likely to make better grades and perform better in school than those who do not. In 1994 in a Readers' Digest national poll of high school seniors, Lou Harris reported higher school scores among seniors who ate with their families. He also found that high school seniors were happier with themselves and prospects for the future than seniors who did not eat at home regularly.

Sunshine Guacamole

4 ripe avocados
3 tablespoons lime juice
2 tablespoons diced fresh tomatoes
1 clove garlic, minced
¼ cup minced cilantro
Hot pepper sauce or minced jalapeno pepper

- Peel and coarsely mash avocados, but leave some bite-sized pieces. Mix all ingredients in bowl.

- Add a little salt, pepper and a little hot sauce to taste and serve immediately. Makes about 1 pint.

God made rainy days so gardeners could get housework done.

Prosciutto and Melon Bites

This is so simple, but the flavors are so heavenly.

1 large cantaloupe or honeydew melon
1 lime, juiced
¼ - ½ pound thinly sliced prosciutto
Balsamic vinegar

- Remove cantaloupe rind and cut into bite-size pieces. Place into container and pour lime juice over cantaloupe and toss well.

- Wrap piece of prosciutto around each cantaloupe bite. Sprinkle with balsamic vinegar and serve. Serves 6 to 8.

> The secret of staying young is to live honestly, eat slowly and lie about your age.
> —Lucille Ball

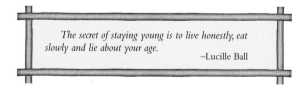

Peppered Bacon-Zucchini Rolls

2 zucchini
12 slices peppered bacon
2 ounces goat cheese or ¼ cup whipped
    cream cheese
1 teaspoon lemon juice
1 teaspoon dried parsley

Slice zucchini lengthwise about ¼ inch thick. Fry bacon, but not crisp and still soft; drain well. Mix cheese, lemon juice and parsley. Arrange bacon on each zucchini slice. Spread cheese down middle of bacon and roll up. Secure with toothpick if needed.

Cook on sprayed grill over medium hot fire for about 5 minutes or until grill marks show and zucchini is tender. Remove from grill before cheese melts. Makes about 12 rolls.

Two cannibals were eating a clown. One said to the other, "Does this taste funny to you?"

Fresh Garlic Mushrooms

1 tablespoon extra virgin olive oil
2 tablespoons butter
¾ cup Italian breadcrumbs
3 cloves garlic, peeled, minced
¼ teaspoon oregano
Seasoned salt
Cracked black pepper
18 large button mushrooms, stemmed

- Preheat oven to 400°. Heat olive oil and butter in skillet over medium heat. Add breadcrumbs, stir to coat and cook about 5 minutes.

- Add garlic, oregano, seasoned salt and fresh ground black pepper and saute until garlic is translucent.

- Stuff each mushroom with breadcrumb mixture and place in sprayed 9 x 13-inch baking pan. Bake for 20 minutes or until mushrooms are tender. Serve hot or at room temperature. Serves 10 to 12.

Garden Stuffed Mushrooms

1 (12 ounce) carton large button mushrooms
½ cup seasoned stuffing mix
¼ cup (½ stick) butter, softened
¼ cup minced celery
¼ cup minced zucchini
¼ cup minced red bell pepper
2 tablespoons crumbled goat cheese

Remove stems from mushrooms. Mix stuffing, butter, celery, zucchini, and dash of salt and pepper. Stuff mixture into mushroom cavities.

Cook on sprayed grill away from direct heat with lid closed for about 10 minutes or until mushrooms are tender and grill marks appear. Sprinkle with goat cheese. Serves about 4 to 6.

Peppers originated in the Americas and seeds were first brought to Europe in the 1490's. Bell peppers are also called sweet peppers because they are not hot.

Tomato-Basil Bruschetta

1 (16 ounce) loaf Italian bread
Butter
6 - 8 roma tomatoes, minced, drained
4 - 5 cloves garlic, peeled, minced
3 - 4 tablespoons minced plus several leaves
     fresh basil
Virgin olive oil

- Preheat oven to 300°. Slice bread in thick pieces, butter one side and lay, buttered side up on sprayed baking sheet. Bake until slices are crispy.

- Drain chopped tomatoes again and place in small bowl. Add garlic, basil, a little salt and pepper and just enough olive oil to coat all ingredients. Stir to mix well.

- Place several tablespoons tomato mixture on each bread slice just before serving. Garnish with whole basil leaves. Serves 6 to 8.

TIP: *If you like lots of ingredients on bread, double the recipe. Taste the tomato mixture for the right seasonings.*

Island Fruit Smoothie

½ cup low-fat milk or soy milk
1 (6 ounce) carton low-fat vanilla yogurt
1 banana, quartered
1 cup fresh blueberries or blackberries
1 cup sliced fresh strawberries or raspberries

Combine all ingredients in blender. Process until smooth. Makes 2 smoothies.

TIP: Use low-fat milk, yogurt, soy milk and tofu instead of whole milk for smoothies. There is no difference in the taste and flavor of smoothies.

Raw foods have more enzymes, nutrients and vitamins than cooked foods. You eat less than you eat of cooked foods, but you feel fuller with raw foods and are getting more nutrition.

Summertime Fresh Lemonade

14 - 16 ripe lemons
1½ - 2 cups sugar

Roll lemons on counter top and squeeze lemon juice into large pitcher with 2 to 3 quarts cold water.

Add sugar to taste and stir well. Serve over ice. Store in refrigerator. Serves 12.

TIP: Roll lemons on countertop before squeezing to get a little more juice.

People who eat raw foods usually have more energy, stamina and are better able to fight health problems. Most people who eat raw foods sleep better, think more clearly and go through their days more happily.

Gazpacho in a Glass

3 large tomatoes, quartered
1 (16 ounce) can tomato juice, chilled
½ cup vegetable stock, chilled
1 green bell pepper, cored, quartered
1 small onion, peeled, quartered
½ medium cucumber, peeled, sliced
¼ cup red wine vinegar
½ teaspoon garlic powder

- Puree tomatoes in blender. Add remaining ingredients except garlic powder and blend for about 20 seconds.

- Taste mixture and season with a little garlic powder, salt and pepper. Taste again and adjust seasonings, if needed. Refrigerate for about 30 minutes. Makes 3 to 4 servings.

Nine out of every ten tomatoes grown in the U.S. are grown in California. In addition over 85% of all home gardeners in the U.S. grow tomatoes.

Green Gorilla

Don't let the color throw you. This is delicious and so full of nutrition. Fruit masks the taste of vegetables so don't tell the kids about the veggies.

2 cups fresh spinach, stemmed
1 medium ripe avocado, peeled, pitted
¾ cup frozen mango slices
¾ cup frozen pineapple chunks or kiwifruit halves

- Pour ¾ cup water and 4 ice cubes into blender and add all ingredients.

- Process until smooth and serve immediately. Makes 2 smoothies.

Laughing is good exercise. It's like jogging on the inside.
                                                    –Anonymous

Sangria Salud

1 (1 liter) bottle red table wine
1 (10 ounce) bottle sparkling water
Juice of 1 lemon
Juice of 1 orange
¼ - ½ cup sugar
Strawberries
Orange slices
Lemon slices
Lime slices

Pour red wine, sparkling water, 1 cup water and juices of 1 lemon and 1 orange in large pitcher. Add sugar to taste.

Put most of fruit slices in pitcher and set aside some for individual glasses. Pour into wine glasses and garnish with fruit slices. Serves 8.

"Brain freeze" was invented in 1994 by 7-Eleven® to explain the pain one feels when drinking a Slurpee too fast. The medical term is sphenopalatine ganglioneuralgia. It's also called ice cream headache.

Peach Preserves

1 - 1½ pounds (underripe) peaches
1½ - 2 cups sugar

Peel and slice enough peaches to equal 3 cups. Cook with ¼ cup water in large saucepan over medium heat, stir frequently, for about 5 minutes or until barely tender.

Drain juice into measuring cup and pour into second saucepan. Add 2 cups sugar for 1 cup juice. Boil juice, stirring constantly, until sugar spins a thread.

Add peaches; boil rapidly for 4 to 5 minutes. Remove from heat; skim if necessary. Pour into sterilized jars★ to within ½ inch of top, wipe rims clean and screw on lids.

Place jars in water bath★★ to cover, heat in boiling water for at least 10 minutes and cool before tightening lids completely. Let cool overnight and check lids for proper sealing. Makes about 3 pints.

★ Sterilize jars in boiling water for 5 minutes and sterilize flat lids in simmering water for 3 minutes. Use while still hot or warm/

★★ Use a water canner with rack or a soup pot with a towel in the bottom to cushion and separate jars so boiling water has room to circulate.

Easy Strawberry Preserves

2 (1 quart) cartons strawberries, stemmed
7 cups sugar
1 teaspoon Epsom salt

🍅 Finely chop enough strawberries to equal 4 cups and pour into large saucepan. Add sugar and Epsom salt, stir frequently, cook over medium heat for about 10 minutes.

🍅 Skim foam off top. Pour into hot sterilized jars★ to within ½ inch of top, wipe rims clean and screw on lids.

🍅 Place jars in water bath★★ to cover and heat in boiling water for at least 10 minutes. Cool before tightening lids completely. Makes about 4 pints.

★ Sterilize jars in boiling water for 5 minutes and sterilize flat lids in simmering water for 3 minutes. Use while still hot or warm.

★★ Use a water canner with rack or a soup pot with a towel in the bottom to cushion and separate jars so boiling water has room to circulate.

Shrimp and Avocado Stuffed Omelet

6 large eggs
½ cup milk
½ pound small cooked shrimp, veined
1 large avocado, seeded, peeled, diced
¾ cup shredded Monterey Jack cheese
¾ cup seeded, minced, drained tomatoes
½ cup minced green onions with tops
½ cup sliced mushrooms

- Beat eggs with milk in bowl vigorously. Pour into large, sprayed skillet. Cook over low heat until eggs begin to firm up. Slide eggs around in skillet while cooking.

- Gently mix shrimp, avocado, cheese, tomatoes, onions and mushrooms in bowl and spread over one-half of eggs. Use spatula to lift other half of eggs onto cheese mixture. Cook until firm on the inside and cheese melts. Serves 4 to 6.

I'm a great believer of luck, and I find the harder I work, the more I have of it.
—Thomas Jefferson

Roasted Red Pepper-Eggplant Frittata

This is a delicious way to serve eggplant for a light lunch and it is rich enough to be served as the main course. You can put it together the day before and cook just before serving.

3 cups peeled, finely chopped eggplant
½ cup chopped green bell pepper
3 tablespoons extra-light olive oil
1 (8 ounce) jar roasted red peppers,
        drained, chopped
10 eggs
½ cup half-and-half cream
1 teaspoon Italian seasoning
⅓ cup grated parmesan cheese

- Preheat oven to 325°.

- Cook eggplant and bell pepper in oil in skillet for 2 to 3 minutes, just until tender. Stir in roasted red peppers.

Continued next page…

Continued from previous page…

- Combine eggs, half-and-half cream,
  1 teaspoon salt, Italian seasoning and
  ¼ teaspoon pepper in bowl and beat just
  until they blend well.

- Add eggplant-pepper mixture to egg-cream
  mixture. Pour into sprayed 10-inch deep-
  dish pie pan. Cover and bake for about
  15 minutes or until center sets.

- Uncover and sprinkle parmesan cheese over
  top. Return to oven for about 5 minutes,
  just until cheese melts slightly. Cut into
  wedges to serve. Serves 6.

TIP: *Add ⅓ to ½ cup chopped small asparagus
     spears, if you like.*

---

*Frittatas are very similar to omelets with a few
exceptions. Additional raw ingredients are added to the egg
mixture before it goes in the skillet rather than added after
the omelet cooks a little. The frittata is not folded over like
an omelet, but it is completely turned over. The frittata
cooks over a much lower heat for a longer time, around
10 to 15 minutes instead of 5 minutes for an omelet.*

Asparagus Quiche

1 (9 inch) frozen piecrust
¼ cup (½ stick) butter
3 tablespoons flour
1½ cups milk
4 eggs
1 pound fresh asparagus, trimmed, chopped
½ cup shredded Swiss cheese
¼ cup breadcrumbs

Preheat oven to 450°. Place several sheets of heavy-duty foil in piecrust and over edge. Bake for about 5 minutes. Remove from oven, discard foil and bake for additional 5 minutes.

Melt butter in saucepan and stir in flour and a little salt. Stir to dissolve all lumps. Cook over medium heat and gradually pour in milk. Continue to stir until mixture thickens.

Add remaining ingredients except breadcrumbs and beat. Pour into piecrust and sprinkle breadcrumbs over quiche.

Continued next page…

Continued from previous page…

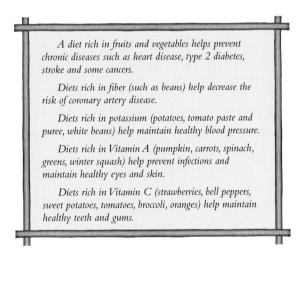

Bake for about 30 minutes or until knife inserted in center comes out clean. Cool slightly, slice into wedges and serve warm. Serves 6.

A diet rich in fruits and vegetables helps prevent chronic diseases such as heart disease, type 2 diabetes, stroke and some cancers.

Diets rich in fiber (such as beans) help decrease the risk of coronary artery disease.

Diets rich in potassium (potatoes, tomato paste and puree, white beans) help maintain healthy blood pressure.

Diets rich in Vitamin A (pumpkin, carrots, spinach, greens, winter squash) help prevent infections and maintain healthy eyes and skin.

Diets rich in Vitamin C (strawberries, bell peppers, sweet potatoes, tomatoes, broccoli, oranges) help maintain healthy teeth and gums.

Robyn Mackenzie/Shutterstock.com

Zucchini Quiche

1 (9 inch) frozen piecrust
¼ cup (½ stick) butter
3 tablespoons flour
1½ cups milk
4 eggs
1 pound zucchini, chopped
½ cup shredded Swiss cheese
¼ cup breadcrumbs

- Preheat oven to 450°. Place heavy-duty foil over edge of piecrust. Bake for about 5 minutes. Remove from oven, discard foil and bake for additional 5 minutes.

- Melt butter in saucepan and stir in flour and a little salt. Stir to dissolve all lumps. Cook over medium heat and gradually pour in milk. Continue to stir until mixture thickens.

- Add remaining ingredients except breadcrumbs and beat. Pour into piecrust and sprinkle breadcrumbs over quiche.

- Bake for about 30 minutes or until knife inserted in center comes out clean. Cool slightly, slice into wedges and serve warm. Serves 6.

Baked Bananas

4 firm bananas
¾ cup (1½ sticks) butter, melted
¾ cup packed brown sugar
1 teaspoon vanilla

 Preheat oven to 350°.

 Halve bananas lengthwise and peel each half carefully; set aside the peels for presentation. Slice the bananas and arrange in sprayed baking dish.

 In saucepan, combine butter and brown sugar and heat just enough to mix well. Stir in vanilla and pour over bananas.

 Bake for 15 to 20 minutes or until bananas are soft and sauce is bubbling. Arrange the banana slices in the peels to serve. Serves 8.

Why are bananas never lonely?
Because they hang around in bunches.

Why did the banana go out with a prune?
Because he couldn't get a date.

MnemosyneM/Shutterstock.com

Breakfast Fruit Parfait

Red huckleberries are always called huckleberries, but other species may be called blueberries or huckleberries depending on local custom.

1 cup flavored or plain yogurt
1 tablespoon honey
½ cup granola cereal
2 cups sliced fresh fruit

Mix yogurt and honey with granola in bowl and top with fruit slices. Or make as individual servings in parfait glasses or cups and layer ingredients. Serves 2.

TIP: *Chopped nuts are a great addition.*

Honey is the only edible food for humans that never spoils. It is still edible even after thousands of years.

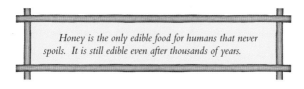

Fresh Blueberry Muffins

1¼ cups sugar
2 cups flour
1½ teaspoons baking powder
½ cup (1 stick) butter, softened
1 egg, beaten
1 cup milk
1½ cups fresh blueberries
½ cup chopped pecans

- Preheat oven to 375°.

- Combine sugar, flour, baking powder and ½ teaspoon salt in large bowl. Cut in softened butter until mixture is coarse.

- Stir in egg and milk and beat well. Gently fold in blueberries and pecans, but do not beat.

- Spoon into sprayed, floured muffin cups (or cups with paper liners) and bake for 35 minutes or until light brown. Makes 12 muffins.

Berries are one of nature's best pleasures. They are easy and fun to eat, loaded with vitamin C, calcium, magnesium, folate and potassium and are low in calories.

Zucchini Bread

3 eggs
2 cups sugar
1 cup oil
2 cups grated, unpeeled zucchini
3 cups all-purpose flour
1 teaspoon cinnamon
1 teaspoon salt
1 teaspoon baking powder
1 teaspoon baking soda
1 cup chopped nuts
1 teaspoon vanilla

Preheat oven to 350°.

Mix all ingredients and pour into 2 sprayed loaf pans. Bake for 1 hour or until golden brown. Serves 8 to 10.

Hard work doesn't hurt anyone, but I don't want to take any chances.
–Anonymous

California Cobb Salad

½ head lettuce, shredded or torn

½ - 1 head romaine, shredded or torn

1 boneless, skinless chicken breast half,
     cooked, sliced

6 strips bacon, cooked crisp, crumbled

2 eggs, hard-boiled, chopped

2 large tomatoes, chopped, drained

¾ cup plus 2 tablespoons crumbled Roquefort®
     cheese, divided

1 large avocado

3 green onions with tops, chopped

Mix lettuce and romaine in large salad bowl
or make 6 to 8 individual salads. Arrange
chicken on top of greens in one area.
Repeat with separate areas of bacon, eggs,
tomatoes and ¾ cup Roquefort® cheese.

Peel and slice avocado and arrange slices in
center. Sprinkle remaining Roquefort® and
green onions over top. Serve with Cobb
Salad Dressing (next page) or your favorite
salad dressing.

Continued next page…

Continued from previous page…

Cobb Salad Dressing:

¾ cup salad oil
¼ cup olive oil
¼ cup red wine vinegar
1 teaspoon freshly squeezed lemon juice
¾ teaspoon Worcestershire sauce
¼ teaspoon dijon-style mustard
1 clove garlic, minced
¼ teaspoon sugar

● Mix ingredients in bowl. Season with ½ teaspoon salt and ¼ teaspoon pepper and refrigerate. Pour over Cobb salad. Serves 6 to 8.

Cobb Salad was created at the Brown Derby Restaurant in Los Angeles in 1937. Bob Cobb, owner of the Brown Derby, raided his kitchen's refrigerator at midnight with his friend, Sid Grauman (Grauman's Chinese Theater). He pulled out a head of lettuce, an avocado, some romaine, watercress, tomatoes, some cold chicken breast, a hard-boiled egg, chives, cheese and some old-fashioned French dressing. He started chopping and added some crisp bacon. The next day Sid Grauman ordered a "Cobb Salad" because it was so good. The salad became an overnight sensation.

Baby Spinach with Strawberries and Almonds

10 - 14 ounces fresh baby spinach leaves, stemmed
1 quart fresh strawberries, halved
1 cup slivered almonds, toasted

- Tear spinach leaves into smaller pieces and add strawberries and almonds on 4 to 6 individual salad plates. Refrigerate until ready to serve.

Poppy Seed Dressing:

⅓ cup sugar
¼ cup apple cider vinegar
½ teaspoon dried onion flakes
¼ teaspoon paprika
½ teaspoon marinade for chicken
½ cup olive oil
1 tablespoon poppy seeds

- Combine sugar, vinegar, onion flakes, paprika and marinade for chicken in

Continued next page…

Continued from previous page...

blender. Process for 15 to 20 seconds. Add oil and process for additional 15 seconds. Stir in poppy seeds.

 When ready to serve, pour dressing over chilled salad or serve on the side. Serves 4 to 6.

VEGETABLES	CALORIES (1 piece or 1 cup)	VITAMINS (Top 3)	MINERALS (Top 3)
Asparagus	40	Vitamin A Vitamin C Vitamin B3	Potassium Phosphorus Calcium
Broccoli	55	Vitamin A Vitamin C Vitamin E	Potassium Phosphorus, Calcium
Carrots	55	Vitamin A Vitamin C Vitamin E	Potassium Calcium Phosphorus
Cauliflower	30	Vitamin C Vitamin A Vitamin K	Potassium Phosphorus Calcium
Green Bell Pepper	15	Vitamin C Vitamin A Vitamin K	Potassium Phosphorus Magnesium
Kale	35	Vitamin A Vitamin C Vitamin E	Potassium Phosphorus Calcium
Spinach	10	Vitamin C Vitamin A Vitamin E	Potassium Calcium Magnesium

Grilled Chicken Caesar Salad

4 boneless, skinless chicken breast halves, grilled
10 - 12 ounces romaine salad greens
½ cup shredded parmesan cheese
1 cup seasoned croutons
Bacon crumbles, optional
Cracked black pepper, optional
¾ cup Caesar or Italian dressing

- Cut chicken breasts into strips. Combine chicken, salad greens, cheese and croutons in large bowl.

- Add bacon and pepper if needed. When ready to serve, toss with dressing. Serves 4 to 6.

The original Caesar Salad was created by Caesar Cardini, an Italian immigrant and restaurant owner in San Diego. When his restaurant ran out of salad ingredients on a busy 4th of July in 1924, Cardini made a dramatic table-side presentation by tossing romaine lettuce with shredded parmesan, fresh croutons and a special dressing. It is now considered an emperor of salads.

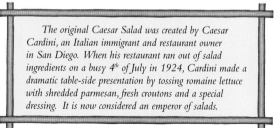

Crunchy Coleslaw

4 cups finely shredded cabbage
½ cup chopped celery
¼ cup chopped bell pepper
¼ cup shredded carrots
1 tablespoon chopped green onion
¾ cup sour cream
¼ cup mayonnaise
3 tablespoons vinegar
3 tablespoons sugar

Combine cabbage, celery, bell pepper, carrots and onion in bowl. In separate bowl combine sour cream, mayonnaise, vinegar, sugar, 1 teaspoon salt and ⅛ teaspoon pepper and mix well.

Pour half of dressing over cabbage, mix lightly and refrigerate. Taste and add more dressing if needed before serving. Serves 4 to 6.

No matter how old a mother is, she watches her middle-aged children for signs of improvement.
    —Florida Scott-Maxwell

Garden Cucumber Salad

2 - 3 cucumbers, partially peeled
½ cup shredded mozzarella or provolone cheese
¼ cup pine nuts, toasted or poppy seeds
¼ cup bacon bits
Salad dressing

Thinly slice cucumbers on 4 individual salad plates. Sprinkle cheese, pine nuts and bacon over top and serve with light dressing. Serves 4.

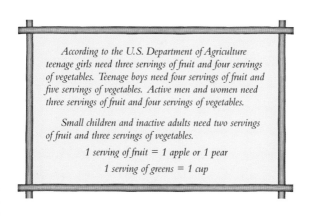

According to the U.S. Department of Agriculture teenage girls need three servings of fruit and four servings of vegetables. Teenage boys need four servings of fruit and five servings of vegetables. Active men and women need three servings of fruit and four servings of vegetables.

Small children and inactive adults need two servings of fruit and three servings of vegetables.

1 serving of fruit = 1 apple or 1 pear
1 serving of greens = 1 cup

Marinated Chives-Cucumbers

1 cup vinegar
½ cup sugar
¼ cup chopped chives
Cracked black pepper
4 - 6 cucumbers, peeled

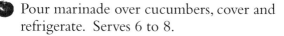 Combine vinegar, sugar, chives, cracked black pepper and ½ teaspoon salt in large measuring cup. Slice cucumbers about ⅓-inch thick and place in large bowl.

Pour marinade over cucumbers, cover and refrigerate. Serves 6 to 8.

Family meals help children learn the basics of good nutrition and how to take care of themselves. Family meals don't have to be big deals, but can be simple meals with basic nutrition. Children learn how to strive for good health and how they are responsible for themselves. Family meals provide a time for family traditions and family memories to grow.

Mandarin-Spinach Salad with Avocado Slices

3 - 4 cups baby spinach leaves or spring greens
4 mandarin oranges, peeled, separated in segments
1 avocado, peeled, seeded, thinly sliced
¼ - ½ cup walnut halves, toasted
⅛ - ¼ cup balsamic vinaigrette dressing

Arrange greens on 4 individual salad dishes and divide oranges, avocado slices and walnuts evenly. Serve dressing on the side. Serves 4.

TIP: Mandarin oranges come in several varieties including Satsuma, clementine and tangerine.

Family meals are great for finding out about your children's lives. When children talk about their day and their activities, you learn what they are learning. You can explain important points and use these times as teaching moments. It is not a time for conflict or strong discipline, but a time for love and nurturing.

Raspberry-Tomato Salad with Baby Spinach

8 - 10 ounces baby spinach, stemmed, torn
1 - 2 cups raspberries
1 cup grape tomatoes
½ cup sliced almonds, toasted
¼ cup red wine vinegar
½ teaspoon dry leaf tarragon, crushed
½ teaspoon dijon-style mustard
1 cup olive oil

Toss spinach, raspberries, tomatoes and almonds in salad bowl and refrigerate. Mix vinegar and tarragon in small saucepan, bring to a boil and remove from heat.

Pour mixture into bowl and blend in mustard and olive oil. Slowly pour dressing over salad, season with a little salt and pepper and toss well or serve in individual dishes. Serves 3 to 4.

The best sweetener of all is the natural sweetness of fresh fruits.

Apple, Pear and Goat Cheese Salad

Fresh lemon juice
1 medium pear, cored, peeled, sliced
1 medium apple, cored, sliced
¼ cup walnut pieces
4 - 6 cups butter lettuce or mixed salad greens
¼ - ½ cup goat cheese
¼ cup walnut-flavored olive oil

 Preheat oven to 225°.

 Sprinkle lemon juice over pear and apple slices to prevent discoloration. Toast walnut pieces on baking sheet in oven for about 10 minutes to bring out flavors.

 Combine lettuce, walnuts, cheese and oil in large bowl and toss. Divide into individual servings and arrange pear and apple slices on top. Serves 6 to 8.

TIP: Sprouts are a great addition.

A fresh apple is 25% air. That is why they float in the barrel when we "bob for apples".

Insalata Caprese

(Salad in the style of Capri – a delicious traditional combination of tomatoes, mozzarella cheese and basil)

2 - 3 tomatoes, thickly sliced
6 - 9 thick slices fresh mozzarella cheese
1 Texas 1015 or Vidalia® sweet onion, sliced,
    optional
3 tablespoons extra-virgin olive oil
6 - 9 leaves fresh basil
Cracked black pepper

- Arrange tomatoes, mozzarella and sweet onion slices in overlapping, alternating pattern on serving dish. Drizzle olive oil over arrangement and sprinkle with salt and pepper.

- Place fresh basil leaves on top of mozzarella. Serves 4.

TIP: *The addition of sweet onion makes this dish even more exceptional.*

Every year since the 1940's, the town of Buñol, Spain has held a tomato-throwing spectacle in its streets. People come from all over the world just for the fun of throwing more than 100 metric tons of ripe tomatoes.

Cold Strawberry Soup

2½ cups fresh strawberries
⅓ cup sugar
½ cup sour cream
½ cup whipping cream
½ cup light red wine

- Place strawberries and sugar in blender and puree. Pour into mixing bowl, stir in sour cream and cream and blend well.

- Add 1 cup water and wine. Stir well and refrigerate. Serves 4.

> *Strawberries are the most popular fruit in the world. They have more vitamin C than any other fruit. When kids eat 8 strawberries, they get 140% of their daily requirement of vitamin C.*
>
> *If all the strawberries produced in California in one year were placed end to end, they would circle the world 15 times.*

Incredible Broccoli-Cheese Soup

1½ cups chopped broccoli
3 tablespoons butter
½ onion, minced
¼ cup flour
1 (16 ounce) carton half-and-half cream
2 cups chicken broth
⅛ teaspoon cayenne pepper
½ teaspoon summer savory
1 (16 ounce) package cubed, mild Mexican
    Velveeta® cheese

 Microwave broccoli in covered bowl with several tablespoons water on HIGH for 5 minutes or until tender and rotate several times.

Melt butter in large saucepan and cook onion until it is translucent. Add flour, stir and gradually add half-and-half cream, chicken broth, ½ teaspoon salt and ¼ teaspoon pepper, cayenne pepper and summer savory and stir constantly.

Heat until mixture thickens. (Do not boil.) Add cheese and stir constantly until cheese melts. Add cooked broccoli and serve hot. Serves 6.

Old-Fashioned Tomato Soup

2½ pounds fresh tomatoes, peeled, seeded, chopped
     or 4 cups canned stewed, chopped tomatoes
3 - 4 cups chicken stock
2 ribs celery, minced
1 carrot, minced
1 onion, minced
2 tablespoons basil

In large soup pot, combine tomatoes, chicken stock, celery, carrot and onion on high heat.

After soup begins to boil, reduce heat to low and simmer for 15 to 30 minutes. Add basil, salt and pepper to taste. Serves 6 to 8.

Researchers have found that tomatoes have a large amount of lycopene in them. Lycopene has 100 times more powerful antioxidants than vitamins E and C. The high vitamin, mineral and nutrient values of tomatoes may help slow down the aging process and some degenerative diseases such as cancers, cardiovascular disease and blindness.

Asparagus with Prosciutto

1 pound fresh asparagus, trimmed
2 tablespoons extra-virgin olive oil
¼ - ½ pound thinly sliced prosciutto
⅓ cup freshly grated parmesan cheese

 Preheat oven to 400°.

Arrange asparagus in single layer in shallow baking dish and drizzle olive oil over asparagus. Bake uncovered about 10 minutes or until asparagus is tender.

Wrap several stems of asparagus with slice of prosciutto.

To serve, sprinkle with a little salt and pepper and parmesan cheese. Serves 4.

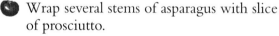

Prosciutto is very thinly sliced ham cured in specific regions of Italy and has been praised for its flavor for thousands of years. It goes especially well with asparagus, melon and mozzarella. You can find it in your grocery store deli, but it isn't a bargain item.

Fresh Asparagus with Citrus Dressing

3 tablespoons extra-virgin olive oil
⅔ cup fresh orange juice
1 teaspoon orange zest plus additional zest
    for garnish
2 bunches fresh asparagus, ends trimmed
½ cup sliced almonds, toasted

- Combine oil, orange juice, orange zest and ½ teaspoon black pepper in small bowl and mix well.

- Place about 2 cups water and ½ teaspoon salt in large skillet (large enough to lay asparagus flat in skillet) and bring to a boil.

- Add asparagus and cook until tender, about 7 to 8 minutes. Drain asparagus on cloth towel and scatter some ice cubes over asparagus to cool.

- Arrange asparagus on platter or individual plates. Pour dressing over asparagus, top with almonds and additional orange zest to serve. Serves 4 to 6.

TIP: *Use both white and green asparagus for an attractive look.*

Grilled Sweet Corn

Fresh corn-on-the-cob in husks
Butter

- Shuck each ear of corn by removing outer husks, but set aside larger husks.

- Remove all silks on corn and spread butter over corn. Season with salt and pepper and wrap corn in inner husks and large outer husks to hold butter. Tie with long pieces of outer husks.

- Place on grill and cook 15 to 30 minutes, depending on coals and size of corn. Turn once or twice while cooking. Remove from grill and serve hot.

If you boil sweet corn, add a little sugar to water. Don't take husks off until you're ready to cook.

Sweet corn grown commercially has yellow kernels. Sweet corn with white kernels and "peaches-and-cream" corn with white and yellow kernels are usually found in local farmers' markets. Sweet corn should be eaten as soon after picking as possible because its sugars quickly turn to starches.

Spicy Buttered Beets

¼ cup sugar
½ teaspoon cinnamon
¼ teaspoon ground ginger
6 - 8 medium cooked beets, peeled, sliced
¼ cup butter

Preheat oven to 350°.

Combine sugar, ¾ teaspoon salt, cinnamon and ginger. Sprinkle over beets; toss lightly to coat evenly. Scoop into sprayed ½-quart baking dish. Dot with butter.

Bake for 20 minutes or until beets heat through. Serves 6.

TIP: *One way to cook beets: Wrap in foil and bake at 350° for 1 hour. Peel when cool and slice.*

Beets are loaded with vitamins A, B1, B2, B6 and C. They are also excellent sources of calcium, magnesium, copper, phosphorus, sodium and iron. The amount of iron is not large, but it is of the highest quality. Beetroot and beet greens are powerful blood cleansers and builders.

Germantown Sweet-Sour Cabbage

2 - 4 slices bacon
1 medium head red cabbage, shredded
½ onion, diced
1 apple, diced
1 tablespoon vinegar
1 tablespoon sugar
1½ tablespoons flour, optional

- In large skillet, fry bacon and drain. With bacon drippings still in skillet, add cabbage to hot fat. Add onion and apple and stir well.

- Add 2 cups water and cook on low heat for 1 hour. (Liquid should cook down in this time.)

- Season with salt, pepper, vinegar and sugar. If desired, thicken by mixing flour with a little warm water and stirring it into dish. Garnish with crumbled bacon. Serves 6 to 8.

Why did the man at the orange juice factory lose his job?
He couldn't concentrate.

Brown-Sugar Carrots

½ pound baby carrots, peeled, cut on the diagonal
2 tablespoons chicken or vegetable broth
¼ cup (½ stick) butter
3 tablespoons brown sugar
½ teaspoon ground ginger

Boil carrots in saucepan with enough water to cover until carrots are tender-crisp. Drain.

Combine broth with butter, brown sugar and ginger in saucepan. Heat thoroughly.

Add carrots, stirring gently, and cook for 10 minutes. Serve hot. Serves 4.

Lettuce, peas, cucumbers, tomatoes and basil are easy to grow. Lettuce and peas are cool season plants and cucumbers and tomatoes grow after temperatures reach 70° consistently.

Homestead Collard Greens

2 bunches fresh collard greens
2½ cups chicken broth
5 - 6 strips bacon
1 onion, chopped
1 red bell pepper, seeded, chopped
1 tablespoon seasoned salt
1 teaspoon seasoned black pepper
½ teaspoon sugar
1 teaspoon hot sauce, optional

- Wash and drain collard greens, cut stems off and coarsely chop greens. Place in large soup pot and cover with broth and 2 cups water.

- Fry bacon in skillet, drain and crumble. In same skillet with bacon drippings, saute onion and bell pepper. Add seasoned salt, black pepper, sugar and hot sauce, if you like.

- Add onion-bell pepper mixture to soup pot and heat to a full boil. Reduce heat, cover and simmer for 1 hour. Taste for seasoning. Serves 6 to 8.

Bacon-Flavored Fresh String Beans

1 - 2 pounds fresh green beans, trimmed
5 - 8 green onions with tops, chopped
3 - 5 cloves garlic, minced
2 tablespoons butter
5 - 6 slices bacon, fried crisp, crumbled
½ to 1 cup toasted pine nuts, optional
Onion rings, optional

🍅 Fill large saucepan with enough water to cover green beans. Bring to a boil and carefully place green beans in water. Cook until tender-crisp.

🍅 Drain water from saucepan and fill with ice cold water to stop cooking and keep bright green color in green beans.

🍅 Saute green onions and garlic in skillet with butter until garlic is translucent. Toss with green beans and bacon and serve immediately. Serves 4.

TIP: *Fresh green beans are so good, try this lemon-butter sauce with another batch of 1 to 2 pounds green beans: ¼ to ½ cup (½ to 1 stick) butter, 1 to 2 tablespoons fresh lemon juice, 1 to 2 teaspoons olive oil and ½ to 1 cup toasted pine nuts.*

Garlic Roasted Potatoes

18 - 20 small, golden potatoes with peels
½ cup (1 stick) butter, melted
¼ cup fresh snipped rosemary
2 - 4 cloves garlic, minced

Steam potatoes in large saucepan with small amount of water until tender. (Test with fork.)

In separate saucepan, combine butter, rosemary, garlic, 1 teaspoon salt (or sea salt) and 1 teaspoon black pepper. Heat until ingredients mix well.

Place potatoes in serving dish, spoon butter mixture over potatoes. Serves 6 to 8.

Roasted garlic is one of life's rewards. Cut the tops off a bulb or head of garlic, arrange several bulbs (with skin) on foil in baking pan and pour olive oil over individual cloves in bulbs. Seal foil and roast in oven at 350° for about 15 to 20 minutes or until cloves are tender. Remove each clove from bulb. Slice and add to any dish, mash with butter or mash and use as a spread. Enjoy!

Buttered Potato Bake

Fresh herbs and butter will make any dish memorable.

4 - 6 medium baking potatoes
Chili powder
¼ - ½ cup (½ - 1 stick) butter
¼ cup fresh snipped fennel or rosemary

- Preheat oven to 375°. Slice potatoes (with peel) about ½ inch thick and overlap slices in sprayed 9 x 13–inch baking pan. Sprinkle with chili powder, salt and pepper. Slice butter and place evenly over potatoes; sprinkle with fennel.

- Cover with foil and bake for 1 hour or until potatoes soften. Remove foil, return to oven and brown on top. Serve hot. Serves 4 to 6.

TIP: *To add flavor and richness, pour 1 (8 ounce) bottle of ranch dressing and sprinkle 1 (8 ounce) package of cheddar cheese over potatoes when you remove foil. Bake until cheese melts.*

Creamed Spinach

1 pound fresh spinach
2 tablespoons butter
½ cup whipping cream

Wash spinach and shake dry. (Leave some water on leaves.) Remove stems and chop or tear into small pieces. Place in saucepan with butter, cover and cook over medium heat just until water is gone and leaves turn bright green.

Remove from heat, add cream and stir. Cook over medium heat, stirring constantly, until cream thickens. (Do not boil or let cream burn in bottom of pan.) Serve immediately. Serves 4.

In 2004 spinach-eating Popeye was given the distinction of being the only cartoon character ever recognized with green lights on the Empire State Building.

Parmesan Broiled Veggies

Change this recipe for the vegetables you have on hand.

Tomatoes
Zucchini
Summer squash
Bell peppers
Eggplant
Butter, melted
Parmesan cheese, freshly grated
Breadcrumbs

Slice vegetables of choice about ½ inch thick. Place in sprayed 9 x 13-inch baking pan. Sprinkle with a little salt and pepper.

Mix butter, parmesan and small portion of breadcrumbs in bowl to paste consistency. (Use more parmesan than breadcrumbs.) Spread over slices of vegetables. Place on top rack under broiler until cheese mixture bubbles and browns a little.

> It's bizarre that the produce man is more important to my children's health than the pediatrician.
>
> —Meryl Streep

Zucchini Fritters

1 pound (about 3) zucchini squash with
    peel, grated
1 tablespoon minced fresh parsley
1 teaspoon minced fresh chives
1 cup buttermilk pancake mix
1 egg, beaten
⅓ cup oil

- Combine zucchini, parsley, chives, pancake mix, egg, and ¼ teaspoon each of salt and pepper, stirring well.

- Drop tablespoonfuls of mixture in hot oil (375°). Cook until golden brown, turning once. Drain on paper towel. Serve immediately. Serves 6.

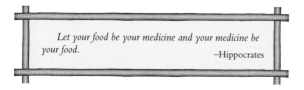

Let your food be your medicine and your medicine be your food.
           —Hippocrates

Fried Zucchini

This is incredibly good!

3 large zucchini, sliced
Cornmeal
Flour
Canola oil

 Salt and pepper zucchini on both sides. Dip each slice into shallow bowl with twice as much cornmeal as flour.

 Drop into hot oil in large skillet over medium high heat and cook until brown on each side. Flip each after a few minutes. Serves 4 to 6.

Middle age is when you choose your cereal for the fiber, not the toy.

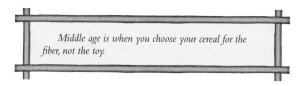

Grilled Vegetables with Cilantro-Lime Butter

1 cup (2 sticks) butter
¼ - ½ cup chopped cilantro
2 tablespoons lime juice
½ teaspoon hot sauce, optional
Fresh vegetables (tomatoes, onions, zucchini,
    summer squash, mushrooms, bell pepper,
    corn, eggplant, etc.)
Olive oil

 Melt butter with cilantro, lime juice and hot sauce in saucepan. Rub vegetables of choice with a little olive oil and place on skewer or grill rack.

Dip brush (or cloth wrapped over spoon) into butter sauce and baste vegetables generously while they cook.

When grill marks show and vegetables are tender, remove from grill and place in serving dish. Pour remaining butter sauce over top before serving. Makes about 1 cup sauce.

Quick Caponata

This Italian accompaniment is a great side dish or chunky dip. It is especially good with seafood.

1 cup minced celery
¾ cup minced onion
1 small eggplant with peel, cubed
3 - 4 tomatoes, cubed
¼ cup red wine vinegar
1½ teaspoons olive oil
1 (4 ounce) can sliced ripe olives, drained

- Combine celery, onion and 1 tablespoon water in bowl and microwave on HIGH about 90 seconds, stir and microwave again for about 90 seconds or until tender.

- Microwave eggplant cubes in 2 tablespoons water on HIGH for about 3 minutes, stir well and microwave for about 2 more minutes or until tender.

- Combine tomatoes, vinegar, oil, ½ teaspoon salt and pepper to taste in skillet. Cook for about 3 to 4 minutes over medium heat until tender. Add rest of vegetables and olives and simmer uncovered until most liquid evaporates, about 10 minutes. Serves about 8 to 10.

Sweet Onion Rings

Texas 1015 SuperSweet onions were bred to be flatter than regular round onions so that onion rings would be more uniform in size. They were also bred to eliminate tears when you peel and slice them. Vidalia® onions, grown near the small city of Vidalia, Georgia are also famous as sweet onions.

2 large Texas 1015 SuperSweet onions
2 cups buttermilk*
1 cup seasoned breadcrumbs or cracker crumbs
1 cup cornmeal
Canola oil

- Slice onions about ¼ inch thick and drop into large bowl. Pour buttermilk over top and marinate for about 30 minutes before frying.

- In separate bowl, mix breadcrumbs, cornmeal, 1 teaspoon salt and ½ teaspoon pepper. Dredge buttermilk-soaked onion rings through cornmeal mixture. Return to buttermilk to moisten and again dredge through cornmeal mixture.

Continued next page…

Continued from previous page...

 In deep saucepan or deep fryer with enough oil to cover onion rings, heat oil to 375° to 400° and drop rings into hot oil.

 Fry for about 3 minutes or until rings turn golden brown. Remove from fryer with slotted spoon and drain on paper towels. Sprinkle a little salt over top and serve immediately. Serves 6 to 8.

TIP: To make buttermilk, mix 1 cup milk with 1 tablespoon lemon juice or vinegar and let stand for about 10 minutes.

> *The USDA suggests that adults eat at least 3 cups of leafy green vegetables per week. People who eat greater amounts of vegetables have higher energy levels and feel less lethargic and stressed. Fresh green vegetables help prevent heart disease and stroke, cataracts, high blood pressure, cancer, macular degeneration and obesity.*

Short-cut Meat Sauce with Spaghetti

1 (12 ounce) package spaghetti pasta
1 tablespoon olive oil
1 pound lean ground beef
3 small zucchini, cubed
1 onion, chopped
1 green bell pepper, seeded, chopped
2 large carrots, sliced
1 teaspoon minced garlic
1 (26 ounce) can chunky garden pasta sauce
½ cup grated parmesan cheese

 Cook spaghetti in saucepan according to package directions; drain, cover and keep warm.

Heat oil in large skillet, cook beef for about 5 minutes and stir well to crumble. Stir in zucchini, onion, bell pepper, carrots, garlic, and a little salt and pepper. Stir occasionally and cook for 10 minutes or until vegetables are tender-crisp and beef is brown.

Continued next page…

Continued from previous page…

 Stir in pasta sauce, bring to a boil; reduce heat, simmer about 8 minutes and stir often.

 Place warm spaghetti on serving platter, spoon meat sauce over top and sprinkle with parmesan cheese. Serves 8 to 10.

> *Pasta has been around for thousands of years, but the variety and sizes we have today were made possible by mechanization. Tomato sauce, for instance, was not introduced until the 1700's and was not used in traditional Italian pasta dishes before that time.*
>
> *Spaghetti and meatballs is a relatively new creation brought to America with the influx of Italian immigrants in the late 1800's.*
>
> *Thomas Jefferson was the first notable American to use a pasta press, but Italian immigrants gave us the wonderful flavors in traditional Italian dishes.*

ARENA Creative/Shutterstock.com

Marinated Beef Kebabs

You will not believe how good this is and how impressive it looks. It is a real treat!

2 - 2½ pounds sirloin steak
Large fresh mushrooms
Green, red and yellow bell peppers
Small onions
Cherry tomatoes
Zucchini

Marinade:

1 cup red wine
2 teaspoons Worcestershire sauce
2 teaspoons garlic powder
1 cup canola oil
¼ cup ketchup
2 teaspoons sugar
2 tablespoons vinegar
1 teaspoon marjoram
1 teaspoon rosemary
½ teaspoon seasoned pepper

- Cut meat into 1½ to 2-inch pieces and quarter bell peppers. Halve onions and cherry tomatoes. Slice zucchini.

Continued next page…

Continued from previous page...

 Mix all marinade ingredients and 1 teaspoon salt in bowl and stir well. Marinate steak for 3 to 4 hours.

 Alternate meat, mushrooms, bell peppers, onions, cherry tomatoes and zucchini on skewers.

 Cook on charcoal grill, turn on all sides and baste frequently with remaining marinade. Discard uncooked marinade. Serves 8.

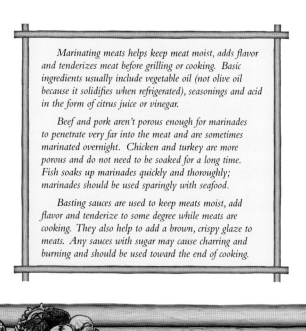

Marinating meats helps keep meat moist, adds flavor and tenderizes meat before grilling or cooking. Basic ingredients usually include vegetable oil (not olive oil because it solidifies when refrigerated), seasonings and acid in the form of citrus juice or vinegar.

Beef and pork aren't porous enough for marinades to penetrate very far into the meat and are sometimes marinated overnight. Chicken and turkey are more porous and do not need to be soaked for a long time. Fish soaks up marinades quickly and thoroughly; marinades should be used sparingly with seafood.

Basting sauces are used to keep meats moist, add flavor and tenderize to some degree while meats are cooking. They also help to add a brown, crispy glaze to meats. Any sauces with sugar may cause charring and burning and should be used toward the end of cooking.

Spinach-Feta Cheese Pizza

1 tablespoon olive oil
2 cloves garlic, peeled, minced, divided
2 fresh green onions, minced
1 (12 inch) prepared pizza crust
1 (10 ounce) package fresh spinach, chopped
1½ cups shredded mozzarella cheese
8 - 10 grape or cherry tomatoes, halved
1 (4 ounce) can sliced black olives, drained
1 (4 ounce) package crumbled feta cheese

- Preheat oven to 400°.

- Mix oil, 1 clove garlic and onions in small, microwave-safe bowl and microwave on HIGH for 30 seconds. Prepare pizza crust by rubbing garlic mixture over surface of crust.

- Squeeze spinach between paper towels to completely remove excess moisture. Spread spinach evenly over crust. Sprinkle mozzarella cheese evenly over spinach.

Continued next page…

Continued from previous page...

 Spread tomato halves and black olives evenly over mozzarella cheese. Sprinkle with a little salt and pepper and top with feta cheese.

Bake for about 10 minutes or until cheese melts and crust is golden brown. Let stand 5 minutes before cutting into slices to serve. Serves 2 to 4.

Pizza and pasta are truly national foods of Italy that have become international favorites. Pizza dates back to ancient Rome, but its modern version began in the Middle Ages when mozzarella di buffalo became the primary cheese. With the introduction of tomatoes to Italy in the 1530's, the people of Naples were the first to use tomatoes on their pizzas.

Pasta Primavera

The Italian term primavera *means spring style and indicates the addition of fresh vegetables to a dish.*

6 ounces bowtie pasta
1½ cups vegetable broth
1 cup sliced baby carrots
1 cup sliced red bell pepper
1 cup fresh snap peas
1 cup (about 6) fresh asparagus spears, cut in
      1-inch diagonal pieces
1 cup grated parmesan cheese
1 cup half-and-half cream

- Prepare pasta according to package directions and drain.

- Bring broth to a boil in large skillet. Lower heat, add carrots, bell pepper and peas and cook about 10 minutes. Add asparagus and cook about 5 minutes. Drain liquid and add pasta.

- In saucepan, combine parmesan cheese, half-and-half cream, and dash of salt and pepper. Cook on low-medium heat until hot. Pour over pasta and vegetables and mix well. Serves 6 to 8.

Grilled Portobello Burgers

4 large portobello mushroom caps
Fat-free balsamic vinaigrette dressing
4 multi-grain hamburger buns, toasted
Burger "fixin's" (lettuce, tomato slices,
     onion rings, etc.)

Preheat gas grill to medium heat or prepare charcoal grill. Brush mushroom caps with dressing and season to taste with salt and freshly ground black pepper.

Grill, turning once, about 10 minutes or until soft (do not overcook or you will lose all the natural juices). Place mushrooms on toasted buns and add "fixin's". Drizzle with dressing and serve. Serves 4.

TIP: Swiss cheese is a great addition.

How does a ghost eat an apple?
By goblin it!

Crunchy Chicken Tacos

2 cups cooked, chopped chicken
1 - 2 tablespoons snipped cilantro
1 (12 ounce) package shredded cheddar
    cheese, divided
14 - 16 corn tortillas
2 - 3 tomatoes, chopped, drained
1 large onion, chopped
1 - 2 cups shredded romaine lettuce
Salsa

Stir chicken, cilantro and half of cheese together gently and warm in oven at 250° to 300° just enough for cheese to melt a little.

Fry tortillas, one at a time, in hot oil for about 5 seconds on one side and fold in half. Hold tortilla open about 1 inch for several seconds more. Turn and cook just long enough for tortilla to hold its shape.

Drain and arrange side by side. Serve immediately with tomatoes, onion, lettuce, salsa and remaining cheese. Serves 6 to 8.

TIP: Buy ready-made taco shells to save a little time.

Homer's Best Basted Chicken

4 - 6 chicken breast halves
Seasoned pepper
½ cup (1 stick) butter
2 teaspoons Worcestershire sauce
2 dashes hot sauce
2 tablespoons lemon juice
½ teaspoon garlic salt
1 (12 ounce) can lemon-lime soda

- Sprinkle chicken breasts with seasoned pepper and leave at room temperature for 30 minutes.

- Melt butter in saucepan with Worcestershire, hot sauce, lemon juice and garlic salt. Add lemon-lime soda. Set aside ¼ cup mixture.

- Cook chicken in smoker or over grill with charcoal and mesquite-wood fire. Cook over medium-low heat, turn often and baste frequently with butter-lemon mixture.

- (Do not cook too fast or too long or chicken will become dry.) When meat is no longer pink, remove from heat and pour remaining butter-lemon sauce over chicken to keep it moist. Serves 4 to 6.

Bayou Killer Shrimp

All the spices make this recipe an all-time Cajun favorite!

2 tablespoons garlic powder
2 tablespoons onion powder
2 tablespoons chili powder
1 - 2 teaspoons cayenne pepper
3 - 4 lemons, quartered
4 - 5 pounds medium shrimp, shelled, cleaned
Bell peppers, onion, zucchini, tomatoes

Mix garlic powder, onion powder, chili powder, cayenne, and 1 tablespoon each of salt and pepper in small bowl or shaker.

Squeeze a little lemon juice over shrimp. Sprinkle generously with seasoning mixture and place on skewers with vegetable pieces.

Grill over medium-low fire and turn once or twice until done. Serve immediately with remaining lemon. Serves 4.

Sweet Carrot Cake

2 cups flour, sifted
2 cups sugar
1 teaspoon baking powder
1 teaspoon baking soda
1 teaspoon ground cinnamon
4 eggs
1½ cups vegetable oil
2 cups grated carrots

- Preheat oven to 350°.

- Sift ¼ teaspoon salt and dry ingredients in mixing bowl.

- In separate bowl, blend eggs and vegetable oil. Add dry ingredients and mix thoroughly. Stir in carrots.

Continued next page…

Carrots are the sweetest vegetable except sugar beets. Because carrots were so readily available, peasants in the Middle Ages made sweet cakes out of carrots. During World War II, Britain's rationing of sugar made carrot cakes a standard. During the 1960's in the U.S. carrot cake was a fad. Today it is a favorite dessert with cream cheese icing, white icing or a glaze.

Continued from previous page…

 Pour into 3 sprayed, floured 9-inch layer cake pans and bake for 30 to 40 minutes.

Icing for Carrot Cake:

1 (8 ounce) package cream cheese, softened
½ cup (1 stick) butter
1 teaspoon vanilla
1 (16 ounce) package powdered sugar
1 cup chopped pecans

 Beat cream cheese and butter in bowl. Add vanilla and powdered sugar. Frost layers and stack; frost and top and sides of cake. Sprinkle with pecans. Serves 10 to 12.

How many times during our childhoods did we hear the adage "An apple a day keeps the doctor away"? As it turns out, the truth is apples are a very nutritious food. They contain Vitamin C plus many other antioxidants, which are cancer fighters.

The Best Fresh Apple Cake

1½ cups canola oil
2 cups sugar
3 eggs
2½ cups sifted flour
½ teaspoon baking soda
2 teaspoons baking powder
½ teaspoon ground cinnamon
1 teaspoon vanilla
3 cups peeled, grated apples
1 cup chopped pecans

 Preheat oven to 350°.

 Mix oil, sugar and eggs in bowl and beat well.

In separate bowl, combine flour, ½ teaspoon salt, baking soda, baking powder and cinnamon. Gradually add flour mixture to creamed mixture.

Add vanilla, fold in apples and pecans and pour into sprayed, floured tube pan.

Continued next page…

Continued from previous page...

 Bake for 1 hour. While cake is still warm, invert onto serving plate.

Glaze:

2 tablespoons butter, melted
2 tablespoons milk
1 cup powdered sugar
1 teaspoon vanilla
¼ teaspoon lemon extract

 Combine and mix all ingredients in bowl and drizzle over cake while cake is still warm. Serves 18 to 20.

Apples are more efficient than caffeine at waking you up in the morning.

It's better to find a whole worm in your apple than it is to find half a worm.

Mark Stout Photography/Shutterstock.com

Strawberry Trifle

1 (5 ounce) package French vanilla instant
    pudding mix
1 (10 ounce) loaf pound cake or angel food cake
½ cup sherry, divided
2 cups fresh strawberries, sliced
Frozen whipped topping, thawed

Prepare pudding according to package
directions.

Layer half pound cake slices in bottom of
8-inch glass bowl. Sprinkle with ¼ cup
sherry. Add layer of half strawberries. Next,
layer half pudding.

Repeat these layers. Refrigerate overnight
or several hours.

Before serving, top with whipped topping.
Serves 4.

TIP: *Individual servings in parfait or wine glasses
    create a beautiful dessert.*

About 94% of all American households eat
strawberries. California produces over one billion pounds
of strawberries annually, about 75% of all the strawberries
eaten in the U.S.

Homemade Peach Ice Cream

1½ quarts mashed, ripe peaches
2 tablespoons vanilla
2 (14 ounce) cans sweetened condensed milk
1 (12 ounce) can evaporated milk
½ cup sugar
½ gallon milk

Combine peaches, vanilla, ½ teaspoon salt, sweetened condensed milk, evaporated milk and sugar in ice cream freezer container and mix well. Add milk to mixture line in container.

Freeze according to manufacturer's directions. Serves 10 to 12.

Some form of ice cream has been around as far back as 2000 BC in China. It didn't really become popular in the U.S. until the 1850's after Nancy Johnson invented the hand crank ice cream freezer. The first commercial ice cream freezer didn't appear until the 1920's.

Ice Cream with Hot Raspberry Sauce

2 pints fresh raspberries
¾ cup sugar
2 tablespoons cornstarch
Ice cream

🍓 Soak raspberries with sugar in ½ cup water in saucepan for about 20 minutes. Pour small amount of water from raspberries into small cup. Add cornstarch and stir well to dissolve cornstarch.

🍓 Pour raspberries and cornstarch mixture into blender and process to desired consistency. Strain over saucepan. (Discard seeds and pulp.)

🍓 Bring to a boil, reduce heat to low and cook for 2 to 4 minutes or until sauce thickens; stir constantly. Serve over ice cream. Serves 4.

The biggest ice cream sundae on record was 12 feet tall and made with 4,667 gallons of ice cream in California in 1985.

Honey Baked Pears

6 medium pears, cored, halved lengthwise
¾ cup honey
2 tablespoons crystallized ginger, finely chopped

🍅 Preheat oven to 350°.

🍅 Place cut pears in sprayed 9 x 13-inch baking pan. Drizzle with honey and sprinkle with finely chopped ginger and add ¾ cup water.

🍅 Cover and bake for 40 minutes. Serves 6.

A group of chess players checked into a hotel and talked to each other in the lobby about a tournament victory. After some time, the hotel manager asked them to leave the lobby. "Why?" asked one of the players. "Because", he said, "I don't like a bunch of chess nuts boasting in an open foyer."

Kahlua Fruit Dip

1 (8 ounce) package cream cheese, softened
1 (8 ounce) carton whipped topping
⅔ cup packed brown sugar
⅓ cup Kahlua® liqueur
1 (8 ounce) carton sour cream
Sliced fresh fruit

 Whip cream cheese in bowl until creamy and fold in whipped topping.

 Add brown sugar, Kahlua® liqueur and sour cream and mix well.

 Refrigerate for 24 hours before serving with fresh fruit. Makes 3 cups.

You can't change the past, but you can ruin the present by worrying over the future.
—Anonymous

Cookie Crust Fruit Pizza

What a way to get your daily fruit servings!
Party perfect!

1 (16 ounce) package refrigerated sugar
        cookie dough
1 (8 ounce) package reduced-fat cream cheese
1 cup sugar, divided
2 teaspoons vanilla
4 cups seasonal fruit, sliced or cut into
        bite-size pieces
3 tablespoons cornstarch
1 cup fresh orange or pineapple juice

🍎 Press cookie dough into circle on 12-inch
  pizza pan. Bake according to package
  directions. Cool.

🍎 Combine cream cheese, ½ cup sugar and
  vanilla in mixing bowl and beat until
  smooth. Spread evenly over cookie crust.
  Arrange fruit on top of cream cheese
  mixture.

Continued next page…

Continued from previous page...

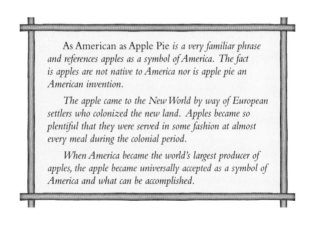

Combine remaining sugar, cornstarch and juice in 1-quart saucepan and cook over medium heat. Stir until sugar mixture boils and thickens. Cool and spread over fruit. Cut into 8 wedges. Serves 8.

TIP: Use raspberries, blueberries, sliced strawberries, sliced kiwi fruit, sliced bananas, sliced peaches or drained pineapple tidbits. Use toasted macadamia nuts to add crunchiness and great flavor.

As American as Apple Pie *is a very familiar phrase and references apples as a symbol of America. The fact is apples are not native to America nor is apple pie an American invention.*

The apple came to the New World by way of European settlers who colonized the new land. Apples became so plentiful that they were served in some fashion at almost every meal during the colonial period.

When America became the world's largest producer of apples, the apple became universally accepted as a symbol of America and what can be accomplished.

Old-Fashioned Apple Pie

The best way to save time with this apple pie is to buy 1 (15 ounce) package refrigerated double piecrusts. Modern conveniences are good to have around.

Piecrust:

2 cups flour
⅔ cup shortening

- Combine flour and 1 teaspoon salt in large bowl. Add shortening a little at a time and stir until lumps are small.

- Slowly pour in 3 tablespoons cold water and stir until it mixes well. Divide dough into 2 pieces and place on floured countertop.

- Roll out each piece of dough to about ⅛-inch thick. Place 1 inside 9-inch pie pan. Save remaining half for upper crust.

Continued next page…

I totally take back all those times I didn't want to take a nap when I was younger.

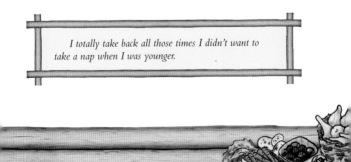

Continued from previous page…

Pie Filling:

2 tablespoons lemon juice
6 cups peeled, cored, sliced Gala apples
1 cup plus 1 tablespoon sugar
2 tablespoons flour
1½ teaspoons ground cinnamon

- Preheat oven to 425°.

- Sprinkle lemon juice over apples and stir to mix with all slices in bowl.

- In separate bowl, mix sugar, flour and cinnamon. Pour over apples and stir in.

- Pour pie filling into piecrust. Place second piecrust over top and seal edges of piecrusts.

- Cut slits in top piecrust. Bake for 60 minutes and cool before serving. Serves 8.

The average American eats about 50 pounds of apples every year. About one-third of this total is fresh whole apples; the rest is in prepared foods such as applesauce, apple pie and other desserts, apple juice and apple cider, etc.

Rhubarb Pie

3 cups rhubarb (about 1 pound)
2 (9-inch) refrigerated piecrusts
1 cup sugar
2 tablespoons flour
2 eggs, beaten

- Preheat oven to 425°.

- Peel rhubarb and cut in ½-inch pieces before measuring. Line a pie pan with 1 piecrust.

- Mix sugar, flour, ⅛ teaspoon salt and eggs. Add to the rhubarb and turn into pie pan. Moisten edge of pastry with water. Cover with top crust. Press edges together and trim. Make slits in top to let steam escape.

- Bake for 10 minutes. Reduce heat to 325° and continue baking for additional 30 minutes. Serves 6 to 8.

In the 1800's the first bakery was started on the yeast coast.

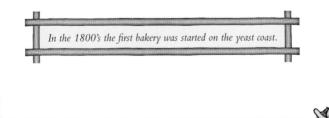

Easy Peach Cobbler

½ cup (1 stick) butter, melted
1 cup flour
2¼ cups sugar, divided
2 teaspoons baking powder
1 cup milk
3 - 4 cups fresh, ripe sliced peaches
1 teaspoon ground cinnamon

- Preheat oven to 350°.

- Combine butter, flour, 1 cup sugar, baking powder and ¼ teaspoon salt in bowl; mix in milk and blend well.

- Spoon into sprayed 9 x 13-inch glass baking dish. Combine sliced peaches, 1¼ cups sugar and cinnamon and pour over dough.

- Bake for 1 hour. Crust will come to top. Mix cinnamon with a little sugar and dust cobbler with mixture. Serves 10.

The world's largest peach cobbler is made every year in Georgia. It is 11 feet long and 5 feet wide. Georgia's nickname is the Peach State.

Bibliography

A Texas Hill Country Cookbook Blue-Lake-Deerhaven Cookbook Committee Marble Falls, Texas 1976

Ball Blue Book: Guide to Preserving. Altrista Consumer Products. 2004.

Ball Complete Book of Home Preserving. Judi Kingry and Lauren Devine. Robert Rose, Publisher. 2006.

Big Basic Cookbook. Revised by Kimberley Beeman. Mud Puddle Books. New York, New York. 2007.

Complete Guide to Home Canning and Preserving. U.S. Department of Agriculture. Revised 2009. bnpublishing.net.

Consumer's Dictionary of Food Additives. Ruth Winter, M.S. Three Rivers Press. New York, New York. 1994.

Easy Cooking with 5 Ingredients. Barbara C. Jones. Cookbook Resources, LLC. Highland Village, Texas. 2002.

Food Lover's Companion. Sharon Tyler Herbst. Barron's Educational Series, Inc. 2001.

Frances Parkinson Keyes Cookbook. Frances Parkinson Keyes. Doubleday and Company. Garden City, New York. 1955.

Great Health Hints and Handy Tips. Reader's Digest. The Reader's Digest Association, Inc. Pleasantville, New York/Montreal. 1994.

I'll Have What They Are Having. Linda Stradley. Three Forks, Globe Pequot Press. Guilford, Connecticut. 2002.

Leaving Home. Louise P. Grace, R.D. Bonham, Texas. 1984.

Let's Eat at Home. Julie Bennell. Thomas Y. Crowell Company. New York, New York. 1961.

Pickles and Relishes: From Apples to Zucchinis, Andrea Chesman. Storey Publishing. 1991.

Rogue River Rendezvous. Junior League of Medford, Oregon. The Wimmer Companies.

The 1896 Boston Cooking-School Cook Book. Fannie Merritt Farmer. Gramercy Books. New York, New York. 1997.

The American Table. Ronald Johnson. Silver Spring Books. Weston, Connecticut. 2000.

The Complete Book of Small Batch Preserving. Ellie Topp and Margaret Howard. Firefly Books. 2007.

The Oxford Companion to Food. Alan Davidson. Oxford University Press. New York, New York. 2007.

The Rituals of Dinner. Margaret Visser. Penguin Books. New York, New York. 1991.

Bibliography... continued

The Ultimate Cooking with 4 Ingredients. Jean Coates. Cookbook Resources, LLC. Highland Village, Texas. 2002

The Vegetable Gardener's Bible. Edward C. Smith. Storey Books. Pownal, Vermont. 2000.

The Vitamin Book. Harold M. Silverman. Bantam Books. New York, New York. 1999.

Washington State Fishing Guide (8th Edition). Terry Sheely. TNS Communications Publication. 2001.

You Can Can. A Visual Step-by-Step Guide to Canning, Preserving and Pickling. Better Homes and Gardens. 2010.

Additional References:

Access Washington: Official State Government www.access.wa.gov/

Ball Corporation. http://freshpreserving.com

Ball Corporation. www.ball.com

Burpee Seed Company. www.burpee.com

California Asparagus Commission. caasparagus.com

California Avocado Commission. avocado.org

California Department of Fish & Game. dfg.ca.gov

California Farm Bureau Federation. cfbf.com

California Pistachio Commission. pistachios.com

California Strawberry Commission. calstrawberry.com

Enchanted Learning www.enchantedlearning.com/usa/states/washington

50 States.com. 50states.com

Garden.com. www.garden.com

Larriland Farm. www.pickyourown.org

Sun World: Agriculture in California. sun-world.com

Texas A & M University. Agriculture Extension. http://agrilifeextension.tamu.edu

United States Department of Agriculture. http://usda.gov

University of Georgia. National Center for Home Food Preservation. http://uga.edu/nchp

Washington Farmers Market www.wafarmersmarket.com

Washington State Apple Commission www.bestapples.com

Washington State Dairy Council www.eatsmart.org

Washington State Farm Bureau www.wsfb.com

Washington State Fruit Commission www.nwcherries.com

Washington State Potatoes Commission www.potatoes.com

Index

Cookbooks Published by Cookbook Resources, LLC

Bringing Family and Friends to the Table

The Best 1001 Short, Easy Recipes
1001 Slow Cooker Recipes
1001 Short, Easy, Inexpensive Recipes
1001 Fast Easy Recipes
1001 America's Favorite Recipes
1001 Easy Inexpensive Grilling Recipes
Easy Slow Cooker Cookbook
Busy Woman's Slow Cooker Recipes
Busy Woman's Quick & Easy Recipes
365 Easy Soups and Stews
365 Easy Chicken Recipes
365 Easy One-Dish Recipes
365 Easy Soup Recipes
365 Easy Vegetarian Recipes
365 Easy Casserole Recipes
365 Easy Pasta Recipes
365 Easy Slow Cooker Recipes
Super Simple Cupcake Recipes
Leaving Home Cookbook and Survival Guide
Essential 3-4-5 Ingredient Recipes
Ultimate 4 Ingredient Cookbook
Easy Cooking with 5 Ingredients
The Best of Cooking with 3 Ingredients
Easy Diabetic Recipes
Ultimate 4 Ingredient Diabetic Cookbook
4-Ingredient Recipes for 30-Minute Meals
Cooking with Beer
The Washington Cookbook
The Pennsylvania Cookbook
The California Cookbook
Best-Loved New England Recipes
Best-Loved Canadian Recipes
Best-Loved Recipes from the Pacific Northwest
Easy Homemade Preserves (Handbook with Photos)
Garden Fresh Recipes (Handbook with Photos)
Easy Slow Cooker Recipes (Handbook with Photos)

Cool Smoothies (Handbook with Photos)
Easy Cupcake Recipes (Handbook with Photos)
Easy Soup Recipes (Handbook with Photos)
Classic Tex-Mex and Texas Cooking
Best-Loved Southern Recipes
Classic Southwest Cooking
Miss Sadie's Southern Cooking
Classic Pennsylvania Dutch Cooking
The Quilters' Cookbook
Healthy Cooking with 4 Ingredients
Trophy Hunter's Wild Game Cookbook
Recipe Keeper
Simple Old-Fashioned Baking
Quick Fixes with Cake Mixes
Kitchen Keepsakes & More Kitchen Keepsakes
Cookbook 25 Years
Texas Longhorn Cookbook
The Authorized Texas Ranger Cookbook
Gifts for the Cookie Jar
All New Gifts for the Cookie Jar
The Big Bake Sale Cookbook
Easy One-Dish Meals
Easy Potluck Recipes
Easy Casseroles Cookbook
Easy Desserts
Sunday Night Suppers
Easy Church Suppers
365 Easy Meals
Gourmet Cooking with 5 Ingredients
Muffins In A Jar
A Little Taste of Texas
A Little Taste of Texas II
Ultimate Gifts for the Cookie Jar

cookbook
resources LLC

www.cookbookresources.com
Toll-Free 866-229-2665
Your Ultimate Source for Easy Cookbooks

www.cookbookresources.com

Toll-Free 866-229-2665

Your Ultimate Source for Easy Cookbooks